Written by Jo Windsor

Look at these birds.
They are parrots.
There are different
kinds of parrots.
Parrots can live
in lots of places.

This parrot lives
in the rain forest.
It lives up in the trees.

This parrot lives
in the cold mountains.
It is not very good at flying.
It lives on the ground.

Parrots have very strong beaks.
They can use their beaks
to make nests.
They can use their beaks
to eat seeds and
clean their feathers.

beak

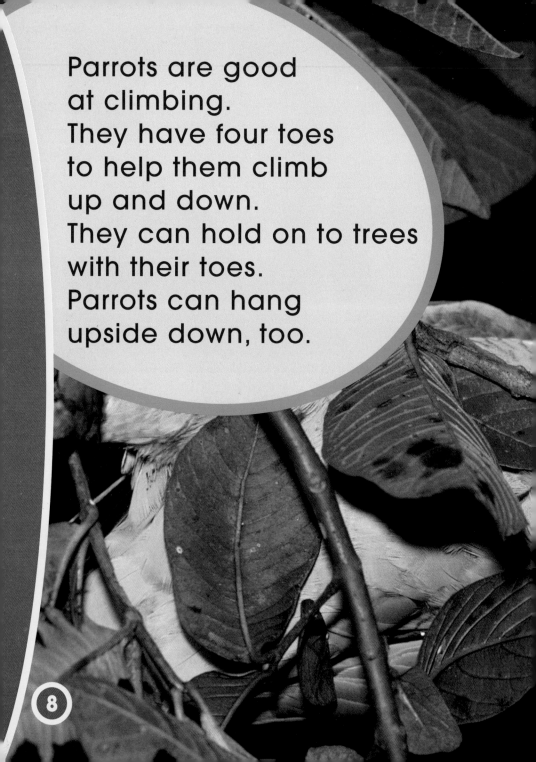

Parrots are good
at climbing.
They have four toes
to help them climb
up and down.
They can hold on to trees
with their toes.
Parrots can hang
upside down, too.

toes

Sometimes people try
to steal parrots.
This tree has a trap!
The trap catches
the parrots.
People then take
the parrots away.

trap

11

Sometimes people steal
baby parrots, too.
They take
the baby parrots
out of the nest.

But. . . people can help parrots, too. This person is looking after the baby parrots.

Index

Guide Notes

Title: Parrots
Stage: Early (4) – Green

Genre: Nonfiction (Expository)
Approach: Guided Reading
Processes: Thinking Critically, Exploring Language, Processing Information
Written and Visual Focus: Photographs (static images), Labels, Index

THINKING CRITICALLY
(sample questions)
- Look at the title and read it to the children. Ask: "What do you think this book is going to tell us?"
- Ask the children what they know about parrots.
- Focus the children's attention on the Index. Ask: "What are you going to find out about in this book?"
- If you want to find out about beaks, on which page would you look?
- If you want to find out about a trap, on which page would you look?
- Why do you think parrots' beaks are good for cleaning feathers?
- Look at pages 4 and 5. What is the difference between these parrots?
- Look at pages 10 and 11. Why do you think people want to steal parrots?

EXPLORING LANGUAGE

Terminology
Title, cover, photographs, author, photographers

Vocabulary
Interest words: rain forest, mountains, ground, beaks, feathers, steal, trap
High-frequency word (new): lots
Compound word: sometimes
Positional words: in, up, down

Print Conventions
Capital letter for sentence beginnings, periods, commas, exclamation mark, ellipsis